Raisin Plants

Introduction	2
The Gardener's Approach	3
Basic Botany	6
Basic Genetics	11
Basic Breeding Techniques	17
Other Breeding Techniques	21
Growing On and Selection	23
A Genus by Genus Guide to the Possibilities	24
How the Hardy Plant Society Can Help	27
Appendices	29

Front cover: *Chiastophyllum oppositifolium* 'Jim's Pride' was found in the garden of HPS member Mrs Frances Pumphrey and named after the gardener, Jim Collins, who had helped for many years; line drawing by John Fielding.

Line drawings by the respective authors.

Further booklets will be published from time to time.
© The Hardy Plant Society — October 1992
Reprinted March 1993 and March 1994

ISBN 0 901687 05 7

Introduction
DAVID BARKER

THE plants in our gardens are products of chance. Even those bred by careful human activity depend upon it, as the section on genetics will show. We can perhaps give chance a nudge in the direction we want it to go, by careful choice of parents, and can even be confident of results in some cases, as in production of F_1 strains. Perhaps in the future, genetic engineering will give more direct control, but for most of us the nudge will remain our contribution.

Making the cross is the easiest and quickest part. More difficult are choosing parents, keeping records and, most of all, selecting from the offspring. It is all too easy to regard our own geese as swans, as everincreasing lists of cultivars of some plants show. I speak from experience: many years of making crosses of hemerocallis, tall bearded iris and daffodils amongst others. With hindsight, I think I would have been more sensible to have chosen less popular groups of plants to work with.

Rigorous selection is the most important part of the process of developing new cultivars, and I cannot emphasise this too strongly. Despite the difficulty of the decisions, they must be taken.

I hope that the booklet will encourage members to try this interesting and — occasionally — rewarding activity, and will guide them on ways to go about it. I look forward to seeing their achievements.

The Gardener's Approach
GRAHAM RICE

ANYONE can raise good new garden plants. Professional plant breeders may carefully plan their breeding programmes, spend years developing and selecting their plants and use all their technical expertise in genetics and statistics as well as in botany and horticulture to ensure that their goals are reached. Some enthusiastic home gardeners approach the subject in the same dedicated and scientific way. But simpler methods can also be very effective and have led to the introduction of some of our most popular perennials.

SELF-SOWN SEEDLINGS

Over the years, vast numbers of good new plants must have been des-troyed by over-enthusiastic use of the secateurs and the hoe. If regular dead heading is part of your routine, as it probably is, most of the seed which produces the self-sown seedlings will never develop. But whenever plants are allowed to shed their seed and self-sown seedlings appear, there is a chance of something new turning up. Hoeing, of course, is indiscriminate and wipes out weeds and seedlings alike. Hand weeding too can be as unselective if you weed in a dream or while concentrating on the music or cricket commentary on your Walkman. But even in the best tended gardens self-sown seedlings still appear and may possibly prove to be different.

Of course removing only the weeds and leaving every seedling in place will soon leave your borders impossibly crowded and disorganised: even at this early stage you must be selective, you must make choices. But leaving a few seedlings to grow on in suitable spaces is usually possible. If you suspect that one is different it can either be left in place to be more conveniently compared with the presumed parent or moved to a nursery bed for assessment along with a specimen of the parent.

So at its most basic this involves gardening normally and keeping your eyes open. But you may like to be a little more selective by dead heading most plants rigorously and leaving just a few to shed seed, weeding everything out of the border that does not resemble a seedling of these plants. This at least introduces a certain amount of control, but is still not very likely to give a breakthrough: you may not be able to pinpoint exactly the origin of a particular seedling. However, there are good plants which have originated as self-sown seedlings in borders and these include: *Erysimum* 'Chelsea Jacket', *Geranium* × riversleaianum 'Mavis Simpson' and also the variegated *Euphorbia characias* subsp. *wulfenii* 'Burrow Silver'.

SOWING OPEN-POLLINATED SEED

The next step from simply allowing plants to self-sow and keeping an eye on any seedlings which result is to collect seed from a particular plant, sow it and assess the seedlings. Over the years this has been one of the most common ways of producing good new perennials and Alan Bloom has raised plants such as *Achillea* 'Moonshine' and *Phlox* 'Eva Cullum' in this way. He discusses the origins of other such plants in *Alan Bloom's Hardy Perennials* (Batsford, £15.99). *Geranium* 'Ann Folkard' and *Kniphofia* 'Little Maid' are other examples.

The seedlings raised from such open pollination will usually either be the result of self-pollination, if you only have one variety of that plant in the garden, or a mixture of self-pollination and cross pollination with compatible plants growing nearby. Unlike self-sown seedlings, you can at least be sure of the identity of one of the parents.

Not all plants are suitable for this approach. Some, like perennial lathyrus, will usually give you seedlings almost identical to the parents. Others like hybrid delphiniums, will often give you a large number of quite good plants, but very few really good ones. But collect seed from any hybrid phlox, heuchera, crocosmia, hellebore, helenium or pulmonaria and the seedlings may be quite varied in quality. Many may turn out to be quite good but not spectacular; some may be horrible; a few may be worth holding on to for long term assessment: in the end one, or none, may really be good enough to name.

It pays to have a plan when considering the plants from which to save seed, and perhaps an idea of just one way in which a plant might be improved. You might, for example, collect seed from *Achillea* 'Fanal' (syn. *A.* 'The Beacon') and look amongst the seedlings for a plant of the same bright red, but which does not fade. Dwarfer forms of existing plants are often very useful and worth aiming for.

Collecting open-pollinated seed from a particular plant at least ensures you know the identity of one parent but there is a way of exercising some control over the other parent without the need for hand pollination. For example, if you have two plants you would like to cross, you can simply plant them next to each other, away from similar plants and let the bees do the work. You then collect seed from both plants and grow it on, some of your seedlings will probably be hybrids. With small plants you could even plant both in the same pot.

SELECTING FROM SEED MIXTURES

A variation on the idea of collecting seed from a specific plant and assessing its seedlings is to buy mixed seed from a seed company and assess what comes up. I recently grew about fifty plants of *Achillea* Summer Pastels (from most seed companies) and noticed that not only did they flower in a wide range of colours but that five plants were much shorter than the others. I have kept these five back and planted them together for assessment and I will also collect seed from them and see what that gives me.

Much of the mixed seed available from seed companies is simply collected from a selected range of good named varieties, so give your seedlings a wide range of blood. *Abutilon × suntense* was quite a surprise when it turned up amongst seedlings grown from a packet of *A. vitifolium* 'Album' bought from Thompson & Morgan. Seed companies such as Thompson & Morgan and Chiltern Seeds list mixtures of a wide range of plants which may just yield something interesting. The problem with open-pollinated seed from your own garden or from a seed company is that the chances of raising a seedling which is better than existing varieties are quite slim. To give yourself the best chance of success it pays to concentrate on just a few different plants, or restrict yourself to only one, and grow on plenty of seedlings — it may be just one in a hundred that turns out to be a winner.

SPOTTING SPORTS

A sport is a shoot on a plant which develops characteristics which are different from the rest of the plant: it is usually the result of a mutation in a bud. Quite a number of good hostas have arisen as sports. 'Frances Williams' is a sport of *Hosta sieboldiana* var. *elegans* for example and this itself has sported to give the all-gold 'Golden Sunburst'. The variegated *Phlox* 'Harlequin' is a sport of 'Border Gem'. These things happen and it is certainly worth looking out for them. But plants also sport to give different flower colours. In the trial of penstemons at the RHS Garden at Wisley in 1991 two sports appeared on different plants of 'Stapleford Gem' and another on a plant of 'Alice Hindley'.

Keeping your eyes open is the only way to make sure that any sports which occur in your garden are spotted. Many gardeners have a tendency to cut off anything that looks different and it ends up on the compost heap. Instead, any shoot which varies from its parent plant in a way which could be interesting should be marked with a label and propagated at the appropriate season. It can then be assessed and if it turns out to be of no interest, it can be discarded. It is worth remembering that variegated sports can vary greatly and even an unremarkable irregular variegation may be worth preserving; it may itself sport to give a more attractive pattern of variegation.

Basic Botany
RICHARD GORNALL

For some readers the following two chapters may appear rather complex and technical. Readers should not be discouraged by the language used: terms are explained. They will find these chapters reveal more on detailed reading.

FLOWER STRUCTURE

When the first flowering plants evolved, probably about a hundred million years ago, at least some of them had flowers which looked rather like those of a present-day magnolia. In order to understand flower structure it is a good idea to begin with a 'primitive', magnolia-like flower before considering others that are more highly evolved and sometimes less readily interpretable. Fig. 1 shows such a flower consisting of a receptacle (axis) on which different sorts of appendage are spirally arranged. In the centre are the carpels: these are pod-like structures consisting of a stigma (on which the pollen lands and germinates), a style (down which pollen grows), and an ovary (chamber) containing the ovules which, when fertilised, become seeds. Surrounding the carpels are the stamens, organs consisting of a filament (stalk) that bears an anther (pollen-containing structure). Outside the stamens is a series of leaf-like appendages collectively called the perianth. In some species the appendages are all of one type, then known as an undifferentiated perianth. In other cases the appendages are differentiated into two series: an outer, usually green or brown protective series, called sepals; and an inner, coloured series, called petals.

During evolution a number of changes occurred, including:

- **The unification of the floral parts**. Sepals can be united to form a calyx tube or various other shapes; similarly petals can form a corolla tube. In some cases, as in currants, the calyx and corolla unite to form a perianth tube (Fig. 2). Stamens can also be united in some species, such as in the pea family and carpels may be united to form a compound ovary (Fig. 2). In some species the compound ovary may be below the point of attachment of the sepals and petals, in which case it is said to be inferior, as in currants and the dandelion family (Figs. 2 & 3).
- **Reduction in the number or size of the different floral parts**. There are numerous stamens and carpels in buttercups (Fig. 1) for example, but only five stamens and two united carpels in currants (Fig. 2).

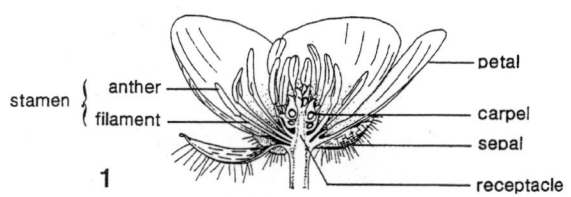
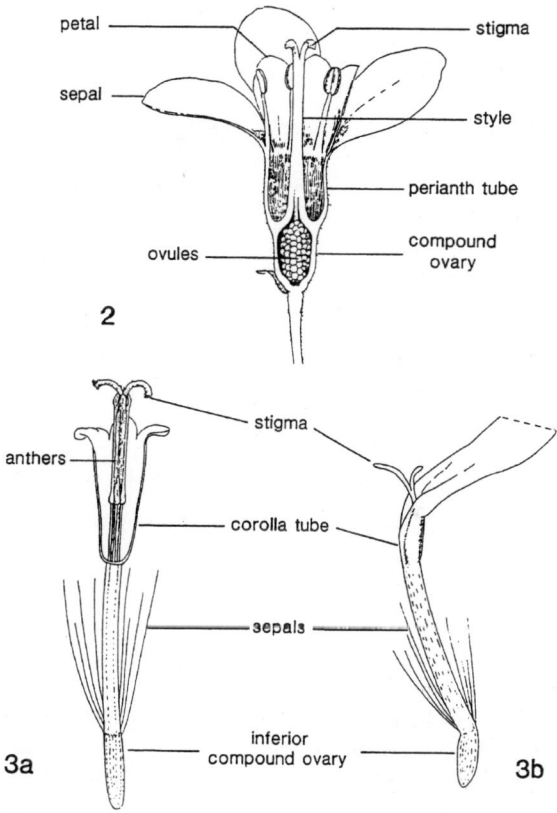

Fig. 1: *Long-section through a buttercup flower showing a relatively 'primitive' arrangement of floral parts.*
Fig. 2: *Long-section through a currant flower showing petals and sepals united in the lower part to form a perianth tube; the stamens reduced to five in number (though only three visible here); and the carpels reduced to two and united to form a compound ovary.*
Fig. 3: *Florets from a member of the dandelion family. a) Disc floret. b) Ray floret.*

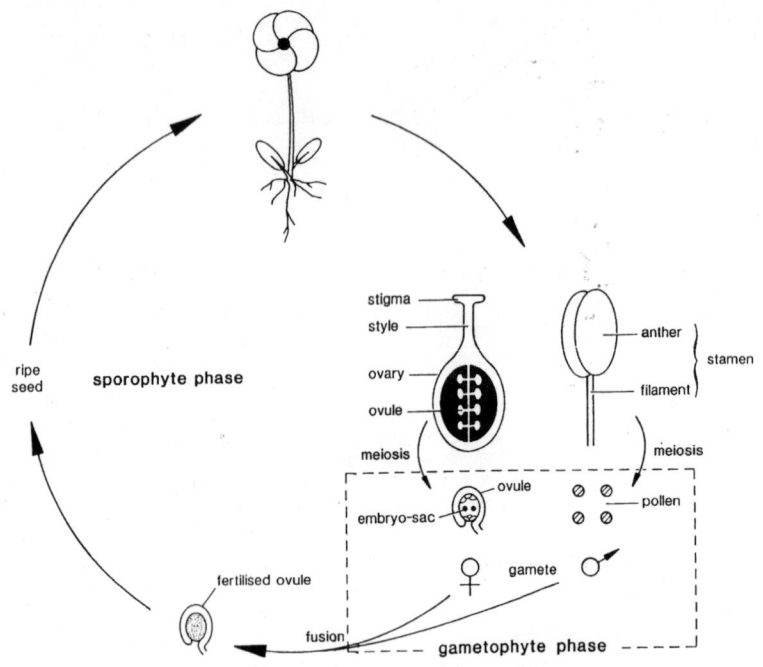

Fig. 4: *Summary of the main feature of the life-cycle of a flowering plant.*

- **Aggregation of the smaller flowers into compact functional units.** Examples of this trend include the florets of a grass reduced and combined to form spikelets and the florets of the dandelion family aggregated into heads (Fig. 3).

LIFE CYCLE

It is important to understand the life cycle of a flowering plant if you are going to manipulate it in plant breeding. There are two phases to the life cycle (Fig. 4): a conspicuous, attractive phase, which is the one we are interested in displaying in our gardens; and an inconspicuous (microscopic) phase, which only sufferers of hay fever appreciate. The conspicuous phase is called the sporophyte, which literally means the plant that produces the spores. The inconspicuous phase is called the gametophyte, which means the plant that produces the gametes (eggs and sperm). The two phases alternate as shown in Fig. 4. The sporophyte produces spores by a process called meiosis (see genetics chapter). The spores grow into gametophytes, which in turn produce gametes, opposite sexes of which mate to produce a new sporophyte. In flowering plants the various stages of this cycle have been given names, some of which may be familiar. Thus the sporophyte is what we commonly refer to as the plant itself. It produces two sorts of spores: those made in the anther are called pollen grains; while those made in the ovules are called megaspores. Pollen grains germinate on the stigma surface and each produces a tube (male gametophyte) which grows down the style. One megaspore in each ovule develops into the female gametophyte (embryo sac). At fertilisation the pollen tube digests its way through the embryo sac to deliver the male gamete (sperm) to the female gamete (egg). Fertilisation transforms the gametophyte phase back into the sporophyte phase i.e. the ovule, on fertilisation, becomes a seed.

BREEDING SYSTEMS

Separation of the sexes. In many species the sexual parts of a flower may be separated functionally in time or space. The stamens may shed their pollen before the stigmas on the carpels become receptive for example. This is known as protandry and may last anything from a few hours to a few days. The opposite case occurs in some species, where the stigmas become receptive before the pollen from that flower has been shed. This is called protogyny, and again varies in its duration. Advantage may be taken of this differential maturation when conducting artificial hybridisations (see below).

Species may also effect a separation of the sexes spatially. Thus some flowers may lack fertile pollen (or indeed any pollen or stamens at all): these are male-sterile. Similarly some may be female-sterile. If a species has only these two sorts of flowers, *viz.* male and female, on the same individual plant we say that it is monoecious, as in alder. If, however, the two sexes of flower are on separate individual plants, the breeding system is described as dioecious, as in holly or mistletoe. There are a few species that have some plants with female flowers and others with hermaphrodite flowers: these species are described as gynodioecious, as viper's bugloss. Other combinations occur but they are relatively rare.

Heterostyly. In a few plant species the flowers are hermaphrodite but the stamens and styles are arranged in two or three different ways, a condition known as heterostyly. In each flower-morph the stamens and styles are separated from one another vertically. In distylous species, such as the primrose, some plants have long styles and stamens that are positioned low down in the corolla ('pin'-type flower), whereas others have short styles and stamens positioned near the mouth of the corolla ('thrum'-type flower). In tristylous species, such as purple loosestrife, there are three flower-morphs, corresponding to long, medium and short styles with two series of anthers located reciprocally to the style length. Successful pollina- tions may normally only be made between different flower-morphs.

Self-incompatibility. Many plant species will not produce seed when they are self-pollinated, as some buttercups. This is not because of sterile pollen or ovules, but is a genetically controlled condition which results in the rejection of self-pollen, on the stigma surface, in the style or even in the ovary. This phenomenon is known as self-incompatibility. Just because an individual plant does not set seed it does not necessarily follow therefore that the plant is sterile; it may simply need a mating partner of a different genotype. (You cannot propagate vegetatively from a selfincompatible individual to provide mating partners — any crosses made will be equivalent to self-pollinations, because the plants will be of all one genotype.)

Artificial hybridisation. The procedure for doing artificial hybridisations is straightforward, although the ease of doing so will depend on the species concerned, and particularly the size of the flowers. You will need the following equipment: fine forceps, alcohol, tea-bags (or similar), lens, and jewellers' tags. The steps are:

- Select the flowers that are to receive pollen and remove their stamens (emasculation) with fine forceps. Wash the forceps in alcohol between each emasculation.
- Protect the flower from contaminant pollen. Empty tea-bags, with one side opened, are often ideal or you can use hand-made muslin bags or even paper if it can be kept dry.
- When the stigmas of the emasculated flowers are receptive (frequently they become moist, or markedly expanded), remove a freshly dehisced stamen with forceps from the selected pollen donor and rub the pollen gently on the stigma surface of the pollen recipient. Wash the forceps in alcohol between each pollination. A fine 'camel-hair' paintbrush may also be used to transfer pollen, but it too must be washed between pollinations.
- Re-bag the pollinated flower and attach a label to signify what cross has been made. A jewellers' tag is often suitable for this purpose.
- Record in a notebook what you have done.

Pollen may not be produced at the time when it is needed. This can be an insuperable problem, since pollen loses its viability after a few days or weeks, especially if it gets wet: some grass pollen live only a few hours. It is possible to keep the pollen of many species (especially those of the rose, primrose, buttercup, lily and iris families) for much longer however if the anthers are collected just before dehiscence and stored in a desiccated condition — in a capped vial with silica-gel. The pollen should then last about a month in a refrigerator and for about a year in a deep freeze; although species do vary.

The viability of fresh pollen (but not dried) can be checked by mounting it in a drop of glycerine and examining it under a microscope. Non-viable grains vary greatly in size and appear shrunken or otherwise malformed, whereas viable pollen is plump and of a more or less uniform size.

Basic Genetics
RICHARD GORNALL

PLANT breeders are concerned with variation, but there are two sorts: that controlled by the environment and that by genes. It is the latter which is important in breeding programmes. To manipulate genetic variability we need to know how it is stored and how it is released.

STORAGE OF VARIABILITY

Genetic variability is stored in genes. These are short chemical sequences distributed linearly along a double helix of DNA, called a chromosome. A gene can be represented by a number of variants, each of which expresses the character controlled by the gene in a slightly different way. So, for example, if we consider a gene controlling flower colour, we could have a variant coding for blue, another coding for red, and another for yellow, and so on. These variants are called alleles.

In flowering plants, the dominant phase of the life cycle is the sporophyte (see botany chapter) — the phase we see all around us in our gardens and in the countryside. In this phase the chromosomes are present in two sets: a basic set and a duplicate or homologous set. Thus the chromosomes are in pairs, which means that each gene in a plant during its sporophyte phase has two alleles present, one on each of the two homologous chromosomes. These two alleles may be identical, in which case the gene is a homozygote; or they may be different, in which case the gene is a heterozygote. In some cases one allele is expressed at the expense of the other i.e. one allele is dominant and the other is recessive. In other cases both may be expressed and this is called additive expression. The particular genetic make-up of a plant is known as its genotype and its physical make-up is known as its phenotype.

Consider a plant with two flower-colour morphs for example, with the colour controlled by alleles of a single gene. Let purple flowers be caused by allele 'A' and pink flowers by allele 'a'. Plants with homozygote genotype 'AA' (remember two sets of genes and chromosomes are present in the sporophyte phase of the life cycle) will have purple flowers. Those plants with the alternative homozygote 'aa' will have pink flowers. Any plant with the heterozygote genotype 'Aa' might be purple (if 'A' is dominant to 'a'), or pink (if 'A' is recessive to 'a'), or pinkish purple (if the effect of the two alleles is additive).

The twin sets of chromosomes are housed in cells which collectively make up the plant body. The plant may consequently be seen as a vehicle by which the chromosomes, and hence the genes, reproduce and perpetu-ate themselves through all time. To understand how this is done we need to recall the life cycle of a typical flowering plant (see botany chapter). The crucial point for plant breeders is that where the twin sets of chromosomes are reduced to two separate sets, during the process called meiosis. This is the point where alleles can be shuffled and variability released.

RELEASE OF VARIABILITY

There are two events at meiosis that are particularly important for the release of variability: crossing-over and segregation. In meiosis, homologous chromosomes form pairs in the cell (Fig. 1A). At this stage the partners may swap segments of DNA with each other in a process known as crossing-over (Fig. 1B). The partners then separate randomly and migrate to opposite ends of the cell in a process called segregation (Fig. 1C, 1D). After a subsequent phase of division of the chromosomes (Fig. 1E), cell walls form to produce a tetrad of four spores (Fig. 1F). It can be seen that each spore has half the original number of chromosomes. Eventually each spore will give rise to gametes, via the gametophyte phase of the life cycle (see botany chapter). These will fuse with others of the opposite sex to reconstitute the sporophytic complement of chromosomes — one basic and one homologous set — and a seed will be formed.

The genotype of the spores depends partly on whether crossing-over has taken place and partly on what course segregation has followed. The processes of crossing-over and segregation are key ones for the plant-breeder because they regulate the flow of variability. Take the example described earlier, of a plant that can have either purple (allele 'A') or pink (allele 'a') flowers. Let 'A' be dominant to 'a'. We start with a hybridisation between a purple-flowered and a pink-flowered parent with the following genotypes:

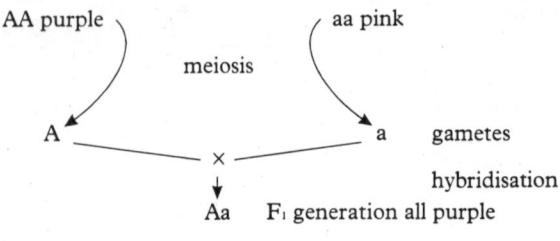

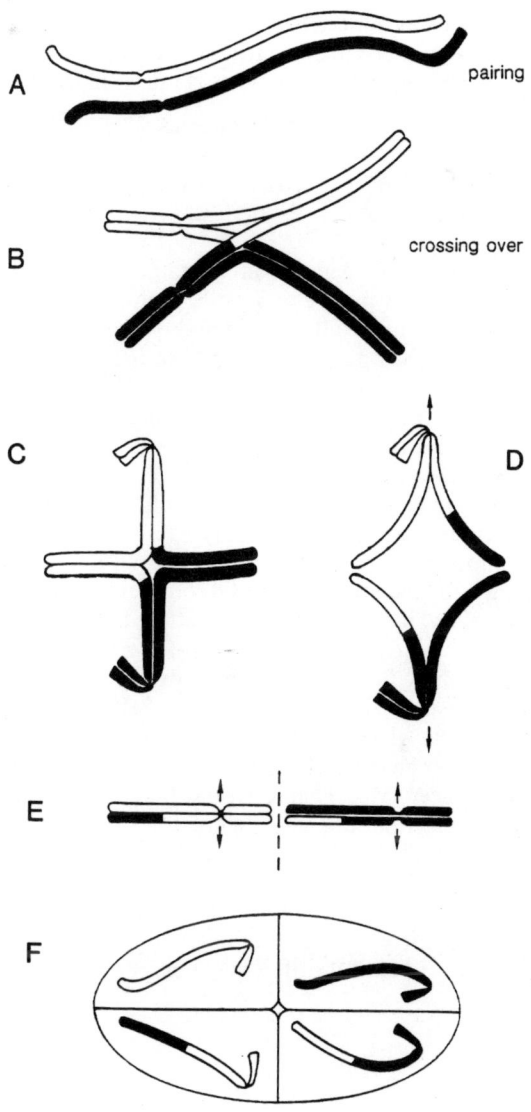

Fig. 1: *Some important stages in the process of meiosis. A chromosome pairing; B crossing over; C orientation of the paired chromosomes in the centre of the cell; D separation of the chromosome partners to opposite ends of the cell; E division of the chromosomes; F formation of spores.*

Meiosis in the F_1 plant produces two genotypes of gamete by segregation, 'A' and 'a'. If these are inter-crossed, either by selfing the F_1 or by crossing it with a sib, the following set of genotypes is raised in the F_2 generation:

		male gametes	
		A	a
female	A	AA	Aa
gametes	a	Aa	aa

It can be seen that the F_2 generation contains plants with a ratio of flower-colour morphs of 3 purple to 1 pink. If the alleles were expressed additively, the F_1 generation would all be a pinkish purple, and the F_2 plants would consist of a ratio of 1 purple (AA) to 2 pinkish purple (Aa) to 1 pink (aa).

The important point is that genetic variability is stored in the heterozygote condition, and is then released by segregation at meiosis. Homozygote genes, in contrast, do not segregate, but breed true. So, for example, if you wanted to propagate by seed an unusual white-flowered homozygote variant of a particular plant that was usually blue, you would need to self it or cross it with another white one to ensure the production of seed all with the true-breeding homozygote genotype. Of course, if you also grew the blue morph in your garden, insects might easily effect hybridisations with the white morph and subsequent seed would be of the heterozygote genotype and give plants with blue flowers (dominance expression with 'blue' dominant) or pale blue flowers (additive expression). Selfing these plants, however, would recover the white genotypes.

If we now consider an example with two genes, the additional effect of crossing-over can be seen. Most characters like height or length for example are controlled by more than one gene: sometimes hundreds. Suppose we have two genes: 'A' and 'B' with alternative alleles 'a' and 'b' respectively, each controlling the height of the plant. Assume that the alleles are expressed additively, and that an 'A' or 'B' allele causes an increase in height of +1 and an 'a' or 'b' allele a decrease in height of -1. Let us start with two plants of similar appearance but different genotype:

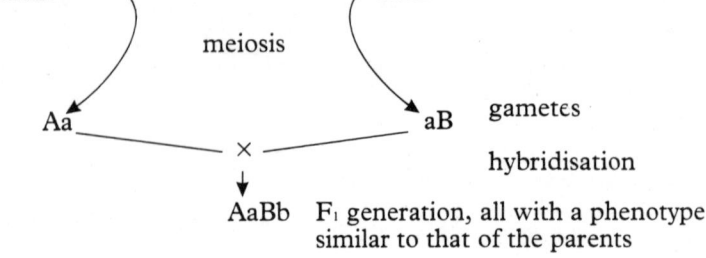

Meiosis in the F_1 plants could entail crossing-over between homologous chromosomes, as well as segregation, so that two new types of gamete for example are produced in addition to the parental types. 'Ab' and 'aB' are parental type gametes, and 'AB' and 'ab' are new, produced by crossing-over: if these are inter-crossed as before we get the following F_2 generation:

		male gametes			
		Ab	aB	AB	ab
	Ab	AAbb	AaBb	AABb	Aabb
female	aB	AaBb	aaBA	aaBB	aaBb
gametes	AB	AABb	AaBB	AABB	AaBb
	ab	Aabb	aaBb	AaBb	aabb

In the F_2 generation there are nine possible genotypes, with five possible phenotypes, four of the latter different from the parents. The example shows the power of crossing-over and segregation in producing a wide array of gametic genotypes, which then mate to produce the explosion of variation seen in the F_2 generation. Not all the variation predicted by this model is actually released because crossing-over is inhibited, many genes are on the same chromosome and are tightly linked together, while completely random segregation of alleles cannot occur.

IMPLICATIONS FOR BREEDING

Where there are no barriers to cross-fertilisation or self-fertilisation, a breeding programme is best started by a cross between two different plants to create as much heterozygosity as possible. This should then be followed by a series of self-pollinations in order to release that variability. At each generation seed is harvested only from the most promising individuals. This procedure is known as line breeding. It works well with species which usually or often reproduce by self-fertilisation. If, however, you are dealing with a species that is a habitual outbreeder, then selfing (where possible) may lead to inbreeding depression in the offspring. This is revealed as weakness or non-viability, a sign of unaccustomed levels of homozygosity. In such cases a limited amount of line breeding is usually possible, perhaps up to three generations. If the weak, inbred lines are intercrossed they will produce a highly uniform F_1 hybrid generation, which often exhibits hybrid vigour. Otherwise, and with self-incompatible species, select similar-looking desirable plants and allow them to intercross. The exercise is repeated with each subsequent generation, until some improvement has been made. This procedure is called mass-selection and involves in part a less severe regime of inbreeding, by sib and cousin matings.

How do you tell whether your chosen species can self-fertilise without suffering inbreeding depression, or is self-incompatible? By experiment!

To introduce a novel character into an already desirable plant the procedure is to hybridise the worthwhile plant with the one containing the novel feature. Then, instead of a subsequent regime of selfings, the F_1 hybrid and subsequent generations should be backcrossed to the worthwhile parent plant.

HYBRIDISATION

Role of parent genotype. Hybridisation between plants of the same species usually produces fully fertile offspring, and a very flexible and wide-ranging breeding programme is therefore possible. Hybrids between different species, however, often suffer various degrees of reduced fertility. Knowledge of this is important if a breeding programme is being planned involving different species — it may quickly run into a dead-end if the F_1 hybrid is completely sterile (see below). So long as there is at least some fertility in a hybrid, however, further hybridisations are possible.

Role of chromosome number. It is a common misconception that plants with different chromosome numbers will not hybridise. This is not necessarily true because the chromosome number itself does not have a direct bearing on the success of a particular cross. It does, however, affect the fertility of any resulting F_1 hybrid, and this may in turn affect the course of a proposed breeding programme. Oxford ragwort, for example, has twenty chromosomes, whilst the related groundsel has forty. If the two species are crossed, the resulting hybrid has thirty chromosomes (ten from the Oxford ragwort gamete and twenty from the groundsel gamete). This hybrid is sterile because the ten Oxford ragwort chromosomes cannot find sufficiently similar partners from among the twenty groundsel chromosomes with which to pair at meiosis i.e. there are few or no homologues in the two sets. This lack of pairing results in sterile pollen and eggs. A breeding programme would have to stop here, unless fertility could be restored in the hybrid. Sometimes this can be done by the application of the drug colchicine, which induces the sterile hybrid genotype to duplicate itself, thereby creating a homologous set of Oxford ragwort chromosomes and a homologous set of groundsel chromosomes.

Basic Breeding Techniques
JOHN FIELDING

SELECTING PARENTS

As a beginner and especially if you're daunted by genetics then it's a good idea to simply look around at the plants you've got that are closely related; preferably different forms of the same species e.g. *Dianthus barbatus*, sweet williams, or different species of the same genus e.g. *Mimulus* species.

Choose the prospective two that appeal to you and that have some characters that are significantly different e.g. one with large blue upright flowers, the other with small yellow pendulous flowers. Now let your imagination combine them together and what would you come up with? Greenish yellow, medium-sized, outward facing flowers? Something in between seems logical. They may all be like this, or a chaotic range between the two, or sometimes nothing you would expect: with luck you may just get the one you were after.

When selecting the parents the obvious features that come to mind are colour, markings, shape and size of flower etc. Less obvious are vigour, pest and disease resistance, hardiness and fertility. These are characters which may take time to assess unless you are using well-known cultivars.

With many of our garden plants the number of seedlings resulting from one cross can number from one to around fifty — e.g. a single cross of a primrose or polyanthus will produce a pod full of about thirty or forty seeds — and that's plenty for most people to deal with. Of course, the more there are, the greater chance of success; we are talking at this level of amateur work so try to grow on the number you can cope with.

If you just want to dabble, choose something that will flower quickly: obviously an annual or an herbaceous perennial such as a polyanthus or lupin (if grown on without a check); not as in one of my interests, Reticulata iris, which may take between four to seven years to flower.

OPEN POLLINATION

The simplest form of this is to collect seeds from plants that have been pollinated naturally without human interference; the bees etc. have done their work. Given a wide range of related plants in the garden, this could produce a good mixture and occasionally a stunning plant.

The normal result will be offspring of generally poorer quality than the parent, especially if the parent is of a 'refined' sort. Seedlings of *Clematis* 'Bill Mackenzie' are a good example of this. Having said that, many of our members eagerly send in requests for open-pollinated seed from the seed exchange, often chasing the same characteristics as the parent, such as strains of *Aquilegia vulgaris*. I have produced a beautiful little double pink, well suited to cottage gardens, from a normal single batch of seedlings of a *Dianthus* species from the society's seed exchange.

SELECTED CROSS POLLINATION

This is where you make the decision of what pollen to put onto the seed bearing plant, preferably choosing a fresh flower before the insects get there.

This might well produce some of the hybrids you were after but it is just as likely that some of the later insect introduced pollen will have worked as well.

It is possible to control this insect pollination on some very stylised flowers such as iris: by removing the 'falls' as the flower is just opening you remove the platform that the insects need to use to enable them to brush the pollen off their backs onto the stigma (Fig. 1a & 1b).

CONTROLLED POLLINATION

This enables you to be almost 100% certain that the seed you've produced is from the cross you've done. Occasionally and with certain plants, such as *Lilium regale*, apomixis occurs producing seeds genetically identical to the seed parent: the intended cross not taking place. At every stage of this exercise, unwanted pollen, including the seed bearer's own (unless you're selfing it) has to be excluded.

Method. Having selected the seed-bearing plant you then have to choose the flower to work on: a bud about to open, that is preferably not deformed or insect damaged and sufficiently closed to ensure that insects have not been in before you. It then needs to be emasculated (unless selfing) by removing the stamens before they shed their pollen. This can be done by opening the flower up and plucking them out with tweezers, being careful not to burst them. Alternatively, with flowers where the stamens are attached to the corolla (petals) e.g. *Primula*, gently tear away the whole of the corolla leaving the stigma fully exposed.

If at this stage the stigma is fully developed and receptive, as with primulas, it can be pollinated straight away then covered and your controlled cross is done. If however the stigma has still to grow before it becomes receptive, as with geraniums, it should still be covered to keep it clean and checked each day until ready. With some plants this may take several days. If you are not sure when it is ready you could repeat the same cross two or three days later.

The flower selected to provide the pollen should be fresh, the pollen recently released and unvisited by insects. To ensure this you may need to cover the flower before it opens, preventing any interference.

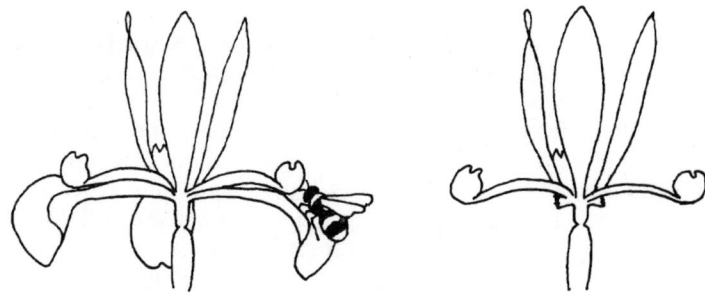

Fig. 1: *Shows iris 'falls' removed to prevent insect pollination.*

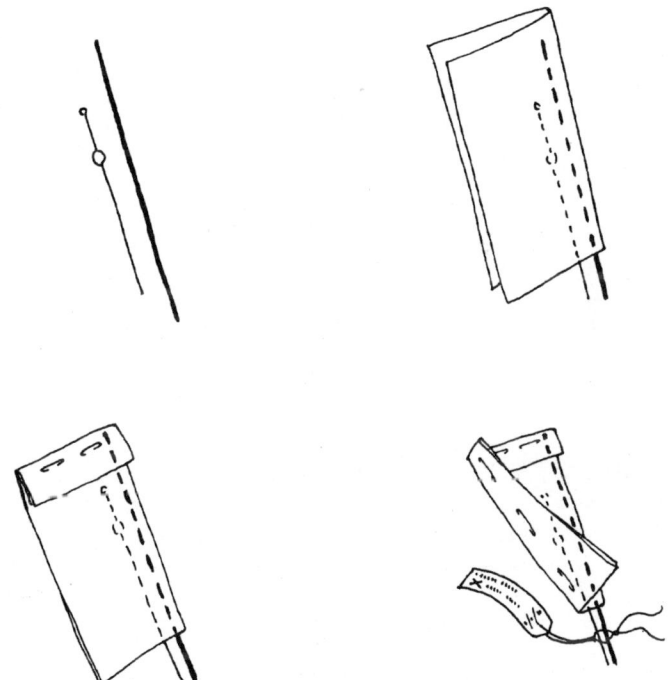

Fig. 2: *Covering the flower to protect it from unwanted pollen.*

Transferring the pollen can be done with a small paint brush. This can be easily sterilised by dipping it in methylated spirits and drying it before re-using. A brush also allows a small amount of pollen to be used on several crosses. Otherwise you can simply pick the pollen-bearing flower and dab it directly onto the stigma.

Covering the flowers can be done in several ways: commercially and under cover it's often done with paper bags. Whatever you use it must be able to 'breathe'. My method, indoors or out, is to use old nylon lace curtains of a plain fine mesh. This will tolerate any amount of wet and will dry out quickly. I take an appropriately sized rectangle and a split cane support (if necessary) remembering that the flower stalk will probably elongate to some extent after fertilisation (Fig. 2). Care should be taken not to damage the flower or stalk so take your time doing this.

As soon as your cross is done label it. This is very important since it is easy to forget what you have used. It is normal practice to write the seed parent first, then the × followed by the pollen parent. Another important practice is to keep a record of what you have done and the date. This will help to remind you of what did or didn't work. More importantly it provides the history of the plants you've produced, especially useful if you start a breeding programme which will involve several generations. In the longer term this will be of use to other breeders and societies interested in your plants.

Other Breeding Techniques
KENNETH TOBUTT

MANIPULATION OF FLOWERING TIME

If two varieties do not naturally bloom at the same time, it may still be possible to make their flowering seasons overlap. Flowering can be delayed by placing a plant in a refrigerator for a week or so while the flowers are in bud or it can be advanced in a greenhouse or on a sunny windowsill. For the pollen parent, a cut flowering shoot rather than a complete plant can be treated in this way.

POLLEN STORAGE AND DISTRIBUTION

It may be possible to collect the pollen and store it until needed. Anthers can be combed into a plastic pill box, for example, with a fine pointed pair of forceps and left to dehisce in a warm room out of direct sunlight for a day or two, or the pollen may be tapped directly from the flowers into the box. After labelling and fastening with sticky tape the box can be stored in a refrigerator, preferably within a tin or plastic container with a sachet of silica gel to reduce humidity, or despatched in a padded envelope to a collaborator.

Flowering plants fall into two groups with respect to pollen longevity. Most have binucleate pollen, which under suitable conditions — cold, dry and dark — can be stored for several months. Others have trinucleate pollen which tends to lose viability within a few days: these include all species of Caryophyllaceae, Compositae, Cruciferae, Geraniaceae, Gramineae and Umbelliferae. A list of genera with binucleate or trinucleate pollen is available from Jean Sambrook (see page 30).

OVERCOMING INCOMPATIBILITY

If a fertile plant cannot set seed after pollination with its own pollen it is termed self-incompatible. And if a cross of two plants likewise fails the cross is incompatible.

Intra-specific incompatibility, comprising self-incompatibility and cross incompatibility between plants of the same species, is common in flowering plants; but it is rarely a serious obstacle to the breeder of perennial ornamentals unless he or she wishes to raise progenies from selfing. Certain tricks have been used to overcome incompatibility. Thus the incompatible pollen may be able to achieve fertilisation if it is applied to the stigma of an immature bud. Success has been reported in the use of mixtures of the incompatible pollen with compatible pollen that has been killed by moistening with alcohol or by repeated freezing and thawing.

Of greater concern may be inter-specific incompatibility, also termed incongruity, as the breeder may be keen to explore the greater range of variation promised by interspecific hybridisation. There are many examples of unilateral incongruity and so if a cross fails it is worth attempting it in the other direction. If the cross fails in both directions there are no generally reliable ways of overcoming the barriers. However, some success has been reported with pollen mixtures as described above.

EMBRYO RESCUE

In some crosses fertilisation occurs but the embryos abort. Sometimes this embryo abortion can be circumvented by dissecting out the developing embryos and culturing them in vitro. Such work needs micropropagation facilities however and a dissecting microscope and so is difficult for amateurs. In rare cases the Plant Breeding Subcommittee might be able to arrange for this to be done professionally.

CHROMOSOME DOUBLING

The classic method of doubling the number of chromosomes, with the aim of restoring fertility to a sterile interspecific hybrid, is to apply a few drops of 0.1% colchicine solution to the growing point of a shoot with perhaps a twist of cotton wool placed on the growing point to help retain the solution. However this method is no longer available to the amateur plant breeder. Colchicine can be purchased only by research organisations or, on prescription, for the treatment of gout! If HPS members feel chromosome doubling is essential for a particular breeding project, the Plant Breeding Subcommittee might be able to arrange for this to be done by a research organisation.

BIOTECHNOLOGY

A number of new plant breeding tools are being developed by research organisations. They include genetic transformation in which a useful gene from one species is transferred to another, perhaps unrelated, species via a bacterial vector, and somatic hybridisation in which a somatic cell from one species is fused in vitro with a somatic cell from another, and a plant regenerated from the hybrid. Although such techniques could generate valuable novel variation they need well equipped laboratories and may never prove economic for many ornamental genera.

Growing On and Selection
JOHN FIELDING

A GOOD EYE

This may be something you either do or don't have; but remember, primarily you are doing this for your own interest, so enjoy it. Many professional plant breeders are throwing away wonderful plants, often superior (in my opinion) to those they are being paid to breed.

Having produced a batch of seedlings from your cross it is important to grow them on in good conditions with the right amount of light, moisture, food and spacing otherwise you'll be assessing them out of their true character. It will be easy to select those you like and those which are definitely not worth keeping; as a novice, the latter are likely to be a very small percentage. You may then have to be more ruthless and cut down on the ones you like to, say, five or six plants. These can then be grown on to assess their performance or continue breeding and selecting.

A plant with good and bad features such as an unusual colour but prone to mildew may be worth keeping for further breeding: if a plant were a true blue rose it is unlikely that it would be thrown away!

Members of specialist societies are often restricted to selecting their plants for features defined in the rules of the society, especially when they are breeding for showing. I find this sad and ironic as many of today's show varieties would never have come into existence if breeders hadn't taken up new features and improved on them.

A Genus by Genus Guide to the Possibilities
TONY LORD

MANY genera have already been flogged to death by the hybridist. Do we really need 50,000 different day lilies? Two thousand *Paeonia lactiflora* cultivars are surely enough and *Hosta* and *Geranium* are progressing very nicely, thank you. But a look at the range of hardy plant species available in *The Plant Finder* shows that a great many have not been exploited at all by the hybridist and offer exciting prospects. Only one species of phlox has really been used to the full for the herbaceous border; just think of the wealth of colours, forms and smells that might be possible if more were used as parents.

But we do not want all HPS members to rush off and start breeding phlox alone: there are many other breeding projects which could be considered. Even smaller genera containing only two or three species offer scope.

It is true that highly bred hybrids such as delphiniums, pinks or chrysanthemums will produce extremely variable offspring and the breeder will have to produce much seed and grow many rows of seedlings to be sure of worthwhile plants. However, many first-rate garden plants are primary hybrids, the result of crossing two quite different but fairly constant species, preferably in their choicest and most desirable forms.

The chances of thus producing a good new plant are much higher provided the parents are compatible. We have only to look at the lists of favourite genera such as *Geranium* or *Campanula* in *The Plant Finder* to see many of the hundreds of such crosses that are among our most treasured plants.

The Plant Breeding Subcommittee of the Hardy Plant Society has already identified a few challenges for would-be breeders. Genera such as *Campanula* are immensely popular with members and have great potential as cut flowers. However, quite a few have beautiful flowers but disgusting habits; hybridisation offers the possibility of more well-mannered plants suitable for the border or for cutting. We would like to see a good purple-leaved sedum, as reliable and clump-forming as 'Autumn Joy' and without the lax and sparse habit of *S. telephium* subsp. *maximum* 'Atropurpureum'.

What about some double wallflowers, old-fashioned in style but healthier and cleaner in colour than 'Bloody Warrior'? Perhaps some hardy salvias with the brilliant colours of the tender species? It should not be be too difficult to re-create Miss Jekyll's old but long-lost favourite *Gladiolus* ×

brenchleyensis by re-crossing the original parents.

On a more general note, with time and perseverance it is sometimes possible to breed or select garden plants transformed in appearance from the original species. Such a change was wrought on show auriculas and, now extinct, the florists' anemones and ranunculus. The striped auricula, lost from cultivation barely a generation ago, has recently been re-created by Alan Hawkes; Mr Hawkes' new plants, beautifully and evenly marked, give little indication that they were derived from a plant with rather miserable ragged flowers and only a few streaks and blotches to show that they bore within them the potential for bold and regular stripes.

The change in the florists' gerbera in the last few decades has been another example showing us how a rather coarse daisy with a fairly limited range of colours could be transformed to give a splendid range of perfectly formed singles and doubles in soft or sumptuous colours. There must be a great many plants which have similar potential if only we could recognise it and we should not discount the possibility of making astonishingly beautiful plants from ones which show only the slightest mutations. These might be characteristics such as a few extra petals, a crimped or indented edge to the petal or a slight streaking or flecking in the flower; with constant improvement, selfing and re-raising or crossing with other individuals showing similar features, it could be possible to create some outstanding garden plants, even from native plants which we tend to dismiss as weeds.

These are just some preliminary ideas; the subcommittee will be looking at many more with the help of experts in the individual genera and considering in more detail how to achieve results. Some other suggestions for breeding projects which the subcommittee has considered and which members might like to attempt are:

- *Amaryllidaceae* to investigate breeding within or between genera containing only a few species and so far little used in hybridisation.
- *Anemone* to re-create double and 'anemone- centred' varieties similar to seventeenth-century florists' cultivars and to select for greater hardiness.
- *Anemone* × *hybrida* non-running forms
- *Aster* (including *A. oblongifolius*) **Boltonia Solidago** crosses particularly for cut flowers.
- **Campanula takesimana** and *C. punctata* hybrids with **CC. trachelium, latifolia** and other species, using best forms and selecting to eliminate faults of the parents.
- *Delphinium* scented hybrids derived from Kenyan species.
- *Dianthus* to re-create pinks and/or carnations striped in three colours, preferably scented.

- *Diascia* hybrids, including with closely related genera such as *Nemesia* or *Linaria*.
- *Digitalis* to re-create most garden-worthy of crosses raised by John Innes Institute.
- *Eupatorium* and *Vernonia* to use good forms of both genera to create showy new hybrids.
- *Gentiana* to use bigger herbaceous species to raise good border plants with larger flowers in a variety of blues.
- *Lathyrus* to raise sweet-scented, large-flowered perennial hybrids in a variety of colours.
- *Leymus* to raise a non-invasive blue-leaved hybrid of similar stature and habit to *L. arenarius*.
- *Lysimachia* to raise hardy hybrids of red-flowered *L. leschenaultii*.
- *Narcissus* to use *N. viridiflorus* to create winter-flowering hybrids, perhaps with the help of embryo rescue.
- *Phlox* to increase the range of border and cut-flower cultivars using *P. caryophylla* and other fragrant species for scent, *P. dolichantha* for long-tubed flowers, other species from Section Phlox such as *PP. buckleyi, carolina, floridana* and *floridana* subsp. *bella, idahoensis, pulchra, stansburyi*, also hybrids of yellow, orange or scarlet flowered forms of *P. nana* (from Section Protophlox) if compatible.
- *Ranunculus asiaticus* to recreate picotee and striped doubles like eighteenth-century cultivars, also perhaps attractively marked singles, using high altitude forms to introduce hardiness.
- *Tricyrtis* to hybridise *T. latifolia* with later-flowering species.

We would be grateful if members could let us know (via Jean Sambrook) about any breeding or selection projects they want to tackle so that we can put members working on similar projects in touch with each other. The Plant Breeding Subcommittee of the HPS might be able to help in a number of other ways described in the next chapter.

How The Hardy Plant Society Can Help
JEAN SAMBROOK

APART from seminars on plant breeding and visits to nurseries and research establishments advertised in the *Newsletter*, the HPS can offer the following services to members through its Plant Breeding Subcommittee:

THE BREEDING PROJECT
- Give advice on suitable/compatible species to use as parents and provide technical guidance.
- Through its Plant Search, introduce suitable parents from abroad, as plants or seed, if not already in cultivation in British Isles.
- Put members in touch with experts on related plants or on aspects of plant breeding.
- Give literature references.
- Arrange the swapping of pollen by post so that members may use plants as parents which they do not have themselves.
- In rare cases, arrange for chromosome doubling of parent plants by a suitable organisation.
- In rare cases, arrange for embryo rescue.

ASSESSING THE PLANT
- Advise whether the new plant is sufficiently distinct and good to merit naming.

NAMING, PUBLICATION AND REGISTRATION
- Advise whether the chosen name complies with the International Code of Nomenclature of Cultivated Plants.
- Provide a valid publication with description and, if possible, photograph in HPS literature. This establishes the originator's chosen name as the plant's only valid cultivar name.
- Register the plant under its valid published name with the appropriate International Registrar (for most herbaceous plants, the International Stauden Union in Germany).

PROPAGATION AND MARKETING
- Advise whether the new plant has commercial potential.

- If so, arrange for propagation to establish the plant in cultivation, or arrange for propagation by whichever nursery will provide the best terms for the originator. In some cases the HPS might be able to negotiate a small royalty but requests that 10% of this be paid back to the society to cover costs.
- In extremely rare cases (likely sales in tens of thousands), members would be well advised to take out Plant Breeders' Rights on their new plants. This is extremely expensive, only applies to certain genera and can only be obtained for plants which have not yet been circulated, so promising plants should not be given away. However, the HPS may be able to arrange sponsorship to cover the cost of this.

Appendices

SOURCES OF PUBLISHED INFORMATION

Botany:

Capon, B. *Botany for Gardeners: An Introduction and Guide.* Timber Press 1990. Written specifically for gardeners and horticulturists with a minimum of jargon.

Davis, P.H. & Cullen, J. *The Identification of Flowering Plant Families,* (3rd ed). Cambridge University Press 1989. Explains the scientific basis of the identification procedure for flowering plant families.

Heywood, V.H. (ed). *Flowering Plants of the World.* Batsford 1978. Well illustrated.

Hickey, M. & King, C.J. *100 Families of Flowering Plants.* Cambridge University Press 1988. Gives the general characteristics of the family and some of its principal plants — a typical example in detail — explaining the relationship between families.

Genetics:

Darlington, C.D. & Wylie, A.P. *The Chromosome Atlas of Flowering Plants.* George Allen & Unwin 1955. Records the chromosome numbers of more than 17,000 species of flowering plants: though not particularly recent, it should be obtainable through libraries.

Jones, R.N. & Karp, A. *Introducing Genetics.* John Murray 1986. An up-to-date account of the concepts and principles.

Moore, D.M. *Flora Europaea: Checklist and Chromosome Index.* Cambridge University Press 1982. A more up-to-date book than *The Chromosome Atlas* (see above) though concentrating on European genera.

Norton, J. *Basic Hemerocallis Genetics.* American Hemerocallis Society 1990. Booklet of three articles from *Day Lily Journal,* of a fairly advanced level, obtainable from Elly Launius, 1454 Rebel Drive, Jackson, MS, 39211, USA for $2.00.

Richards, A.J. *Plant Breeding Systems.* Allen & Unwin 1986. A technically advanced but interesting book: on plant reproduction rather than practical plant breeding.

Plant Breeding:

Allard, R.W. *Principles of Plant Breeding.* John Wiley 1960. An American publication still highly thought of; intermediate level.

Brewbaker, J.C. *American Journal of Botany* (Vol. 54 pp. 1069-1083). 1967. A list of genera with binucleate or trinucleate pollen, indicative of whether pollen is long lived or short lived — also obtainable from Jean Sambrook (£1: inc. p & p).

Lawrence, W.J.C. *Plant Breeding*. Edward Arnold 1968. An excellent introduction to plant breeding though now out of print.

Plant Breeding Abstracts. Work that has been published in scientific journals — and much useful information on plant breeding is never published — can be traced via this periodical. The Royal Horticultural Society, Vincent Square, London (071-834 4333) has it in its reference library, which is open to the public. Various horticultural institutes and universities also subscribe and their librarians may be willing to provide access. (There is a version on compact disc which can be searched very rapidly by typing in search words, such as names of genera, via a computer keyboard.) Photocopies of papers abstracted in *Plant Breeding Abstracts* can be obtained from the publishers, CAB International, Wallingford, Oxon. It can also be worth writing to the authors of interesting work for further information (and perhaps for seeds or pollen).

Tilney-Bassett, R.A.E. *Plant Chimeras*. Edward Arnold 1986. An interesting account of plant sports and variegation.

Watts, L. *Flower and Vegetable Plant Breeding*. Grower Books 1980. Out of print but a useful introductory book.

SOURCES OF EQUIPMENT

Purpose-made pollinating bags, to exclude wind and insect-borne pollen, together with fastening tags and labels, can be purchased in bulk from PBS International, Salter Road, Eastfield Industrial Estate, Scarborough, N. Yorks (0723 584091). Waxed paper bags pierced to provide ventilation or light cages of wire covered with fine nylon mesh may prove adequate. Dissecting instruments, including fine forceps for removing anthers, are available from Watkins & Doncaster, PO Box 5, Cranbrook, Kent (0580 753133).

Chemicals such as colchicine are no longer available for purchase by amateurs.

HPS members are asked to submit details of any new plant(s) they have raised or found to Jean Sambrook using the enclosed form. Jean will also give assistance with completing the form if needed. If you cannot fit all the information about your plant on the form, please use the back.

We hope the form can be used to assemble a register of all plants introduced by members and, if the raiser wants, to provide the first step in the evaluation, naming, registration and/or marketing of each new plant.

Further copies of the form are available from Jean Sambrook, Garden Cottage, 214 Ruxley Lane, West Ewell, Surrey KT19 9EZ or Pam Adams, HPS Administrator, Little Orchard, Great Comberton, Nr. Pershore, Worcs. WR10 3DP.

HPS Publications

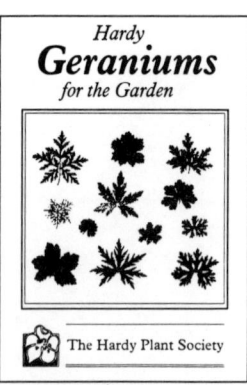

Hardy Geraniums,
44 pages, illustrated,
chapters include:
Cultivation, Propagation,
Preferred Plants and
Specialised Nurseries.
Price £2.50

Hostas,
44 pages, illustrated,
chapters include:
Where Hostas Come From,
Garden Uses, Cultivation,
and Flower Arrangement.
Price £2.50

Umbellifers,
60 pages, illustrated,
chapters include:
Botanical Characteristics,
Propagation and
Umbellifer Recipes.
Price £2.50

To obtain your copy/ies, please send a cheque or postal order
(made payable to The Hardy Plant Company) to:
The Hardy Plant Society
The Adminstrator
Little Orchard
Great Comberton
Nr Pershore
Worcs. WR10 3DP

Forthcoming titles include *Salvias* and *Pulmonarias*